Do you love super silly and ir

(Did you hear the one about the two thieves who stole the calendar? ......They each got six months! ;)

Welcome to the ultimate collection of the funniest, zaniest, wackiest, and silliest math jokes and puns for all ages!

Each page is a new opportunity to discover the best math jokes and puns you've ever heard. So go ahead and have a laugh and share some of these sidesplitting jokes with your siblings, best friends, parents, and even your math teacher!

Table of Contents

Silly Math Puns..3

Number Jokes..15

Questions and One-Liners.......................23

Silly Shapes, Lines, and Angles..............31

Silly Mathematicians................................37

Holiday Math Jokes..................................47

Silly Math Puns

1.) Why do members of the camel family excel in mathematics?

Because math is no prob-llama!

Llama tell you how much I love math!

2.) What is a llama's favorite branch of mathematics?

Llama-*rithmetic!*

3.) What is a llama's favorite linear relationship?

Para-llama lines!

4.) Who is the inventor of fractions?

Henry the Eighth!

I am the denominator of this kingdom!

5.) What tool does every math student need?

Multi-pliers!

6.) What did the calculator say to the student?

You can always count on me!

GO AHEAD AND PUSH MY BUTTONS!

7.) What are ten things that you can always count on without a calculator?

Your fingers!

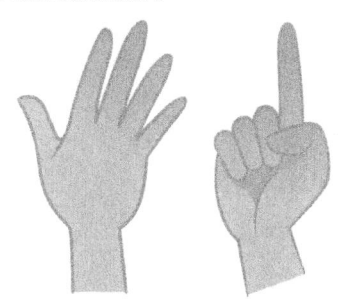

8.) What are ten things that chickens can *never* count on?

Chicken fingers!

9.) What is the most adorable thing you can find in a math classroom?

A-CUTE ANGLE

10.) What insect is good with calculations?

   An account-ant!

11.) What insect is good with shapes?

   Mo-square-toes!

12.) What insect is good with statistics?

   Probabili-bees!

13.) Why did the field mouse change his major?

Because he was afraid of his *owl*-gebra professor.

14.) What does a farmer use to help him with arithmetic?

A cow-culator!

15.) Why is it a bad idea to miss math class often?

Because it keeps adding up!

16.) What do you call 3 feet of trash?

A junk yard!

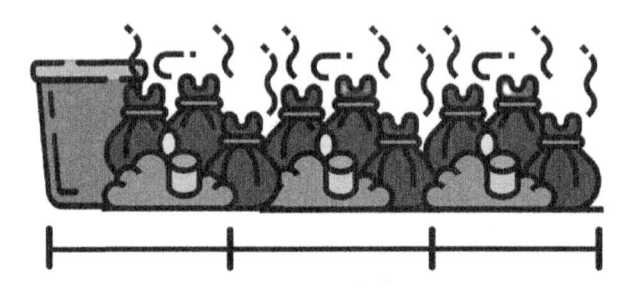

17.) Why did the nickel and the penny start a fortune telling business?

Because, together, they had *six cents!*

18.) Why did the mathematician join the farmer's union?

Because he was protractor!

19.) Farmer Francesca

After a long day of work on her farm, Francesca checked to make sure that her dog returned all 17 of her sheep back to their pen.

> After counting 20 total sheep, she became extremely confused and asked her dog "how do I have 20 sheep in my pen when I only own 17 of them?
>
> "Yes, I know," replied her dog. "But I *rounded* them up."

What does approximation even mean?

20.) A math teacher asked her student if he was any good at rounding numbers?

> "More or less," he replied.

21.) Why was the calendar so worried?

Because his days are numbered!

22.) Why was the hungry clock never accurate?

Because he always goes back four seconds!

23.) Who is the most famous medieval mathematician?

Sir Cumference

24.) Where did he hold his meetings?

At the round table!

25.) What was his favorite food?

Pi, of course!

26.) The Job Interview

Hotel Manager: Thank you for interviewing for our cleaning position.

Bob: No problem! I love to clean.

Hotel Manager: In addition to cleaning all of the linens and floors, you will also have to clean the toilet in every room each day.

Bob: How many rooms are there?

Hotel Manager: The hotel has 288 rooms.

Bob: I'm sorry, but I am no longer interested in the position.

Hotel Manager: Why!? I thought you said that you loved to clean.

Bob: Yes, but cleaning 288 toilets is *two gross*!

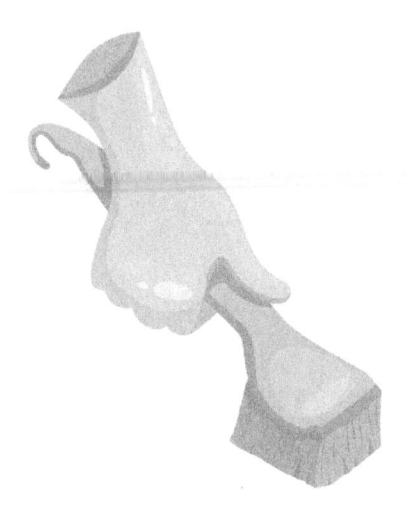

27.) Where do mathematicians eat dinner?

On a multiplication table!

28.) Where do mathematicians go for happy hour?

To the bar graph!

29.) What is the absolute king of all math tools?

The ruler!

30.) What math tool is the most adventurous?

The compass!

31.) Why did the astronaut love noodles so much?

After a meal, he's better at Ramen-*tal* math!

32.) What math operation is most despised by Godzilla?

Kong Division

33.) Why is it unhealthy to make too many math puns?

Some believe they are the first *sine* of madness!

34.) Are all math puns always super cheesy?

Only *sum*.

Number Jokes

35.) Why did the two fours skip a meal?

Because they already eight!

36.) Why did zero and two break up?

Some *one* came between them.

37.) Why did one and zero make such a great couple?

Because, together they are *ten* times stronger!

38.) Why did zero have such a hard time without one?

Because, without one, he is nothing.

39.) What do you call numbers that are always on the move?

Roamin' numerals.

40.) How do you make seven an even number?

Take away the 'S'.

41.) Why did four get denied entry into the night club?

Because he was two squared!

42.) What did 53 tell 47 to convince him to go to the night club?

We're not too old. We're in our *prime* years!

43.) Why did everyone think that three was such an odd guy?

Because he wasn't divisible by two.

44.) Why did all of the other numbers avoid conversing with pi at the dinner party?

Because he goes on and on forever...

45.) Why is there no use in arguing with pi?

He's completely irrational.

46.) Why did five's parents not approve of him dating a fraction?

Because she was improper.

47.) Why was zero jealous of eight?

Because he was wearing a new designer belt!

These are all the rage in Italy right now!

48.) What do numbers do on a snow day?

They go outside and build an eight-man!

49.) Why is the number nine so sassy?

Because she can't *even*!

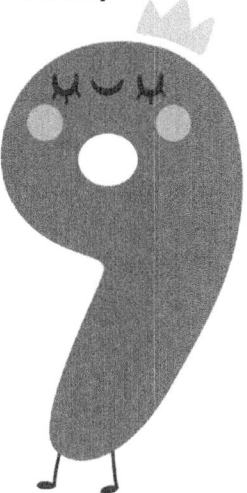

50.) Why is the number zero so frustrated?

Because many people incorrectly believe that he can't *even*!

51.) Why was the addition sign feeling down?

Because he didn't feel very product-ive!

Sum-times I wish that I could be more product-ive.

What a negative thing to say! You're more than enough!

52.) Why was the equal sign so down-to-earth?

He knew that he wasn't greater than or less than anyone else.

53.) Why was the inequality sign so full of himself?

He thought he was greater than everyone else.

54.) Why do squares love the number sixty-four?

Because they think he's perfect.

55.) Why do cubes also love the number sixty-four?

Because they also think he's perfect.

56.) Why doesn't sixty-four believe that he is perfect?

Because he'll never be prime like sixty-seven.

57.) Why was six afraid of seven?

Because seven *eight* nine

58.) Do you know why seven ate nine?

Because he needs to eat *three-squared* meals a day!

59.) Why didn't seven ever get caught?

Because the police suspected some *one* else.

60.) Why couldn't the witness help convict seven?

Because he couldn't really *three* what happened!

61.) Why did one-fifth go to see a masseuse after hearing the news about nine?

Because he was feeling two-tenths!

62.) Where does a round flatbread covered in cheese and tomato sauce with a radius of z and a depth of a get it's name from?

Pizza!

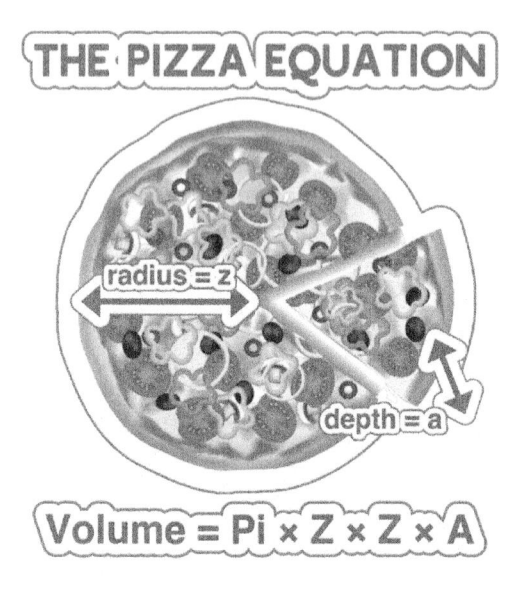

THE PIZZA EQUATION

radius = z

depth = a

Volume = Pi × Z × Z × A

63.) How do people who struggle with fractions deal with cutting a pizza evenly?

They don't. They just eat the *whole* thing!

64.) I want to tell you one more pizza math joke...

But you'll probably think it's too cheesy.

Questions and One-Liners!

65.) Why was the math textbook so sad?

Because it had too many problems!

66.) Why should you stand in the corner of a room when you are feeling cold?

Because it's always 90 degrees.

67.) I'll do algebra. I'll do geometry. I'll even do trigonometry.

But graphing is where I draw the line.

68.) How old do you have to be to drink root beer out of a square cup?

21 in most states!

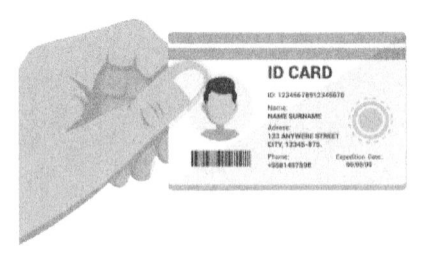

69.) Why is it a bad idea to put 8 ice cubes in a drink?

Because it would be *two cubed*!

70.) What does one dollar and the moon have in common?

They both have four quarters!

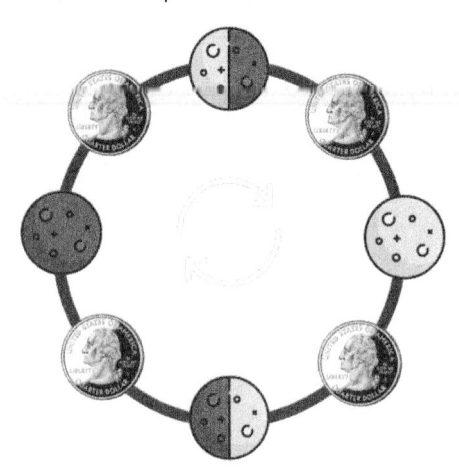

71.) Why do trees hate math?

Because it gives them square roots!

72.) Why do shrubs hate math?

Because it gives them cube roots!

73.) What did the acorn say when he grew up?

Geometry (Gee, I'm a tree!)

74.) What is the most mathematical plant?

A Geome-tree!

75.) What is one tool that you can always count on?

An abacus!

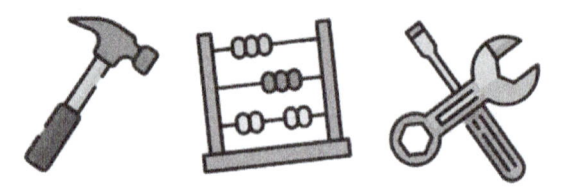

76.) Why can't someone's hand be exactly 12 inches long?

Because that would be a foot!

77.) Cutting Your Work in Half!

Salesman: Sir, this lawn mower will cut your work in half!

Man: Excellent! I'll take two of them!

78.) What is the most mathematical type of snake?

A pi-thon!

79.) What subgroup makes up 3.14% of sailors?

Pi-rates!

80.) What happens when you divide the circumference of the sun by its diameter?

Pi in the sky!

81.) Why does math seem so foreign to some people?

What is 2n + 2n?

I'm so bad at math. It's all 4n to me!

82.) What did the concerned math student say to algebra?

Dear Algebra,

Please stop asking us to find your X.

She's never coming back.

And don't ask Y.

Sincerely,

A concerned math student

83.) There is a fine line between a numerator and a denominator.

But only a fraction of people would understand.

84.) There are three kinds of people in the world:

Those who can count and those who can't.

85.) How come ninjas never talk about how good at math they are?

Because they're ninjas.

86.) How did the man who was obsessed with simplifying fractions think about his past?

Hindsight is 1.

87.) What is one fifth of one foot?

A toe.

88.) What is the problem with jokes about fractions?

5 out of 4 people don't understand them!

89.) What months have 28 days?

All of them!

90.) How many seconds are in one year?

12 (January 2nd, February 2nd, March 2nd, ...)

91.) How would you feel if someone removed the fifth month from your calendar?

Extremely dis-Mayed.

92.) What happened to the two thieves who stole a calendar?

They each got six months!

Silly Shapes, Lines, & Angles

93.) Why does an obtuse triangle lose every argument?

Because he's never right!

94.) Why should you never argue with a circle?

Because it's pointless.

95.) What happens if you forget to close your parrot's cage?

Polygon (Polly Gone!)

96.) What shape is most commonly found at the DMV?

A line.

97.) Why was the geometry student late for school?

She took the rhombus (wrong bus!)

98.) What happened to the square after he got into an accident?

He became a rect-angle.

99.) Why did the triangle drop out of school?

He thought it was for squares.

100.) Did you hear about the over-educated circle?

He had 360 degrees.

101.) Did you hear about the over-educated circle who everyone thought was pretentious?

He goes on and on and never makes his point.

102.) Did you hear about the over-educated circle who didn't care what anyone else though about him?

That's just how he rolls.

103.) What do you call two circles who start dating?

A Venn Diagram!

104.) What is the only thing that flat-earthers have to fear?

Sphere itself!

105.) The Complimentary Angle

106.) Why does everyone like the 45-degree angle?

Because she's acute.

107.) Why was the obtuse angle so sad?

Because he's never right!

108.) Parallel lines have so much in common...

It's a shame they'll never meet!

109.) What do they call the longest side of a right triangle in the jungle?

A Hippo-potenuse!

110.) What do they call the longest side of a right triangle in the forest?

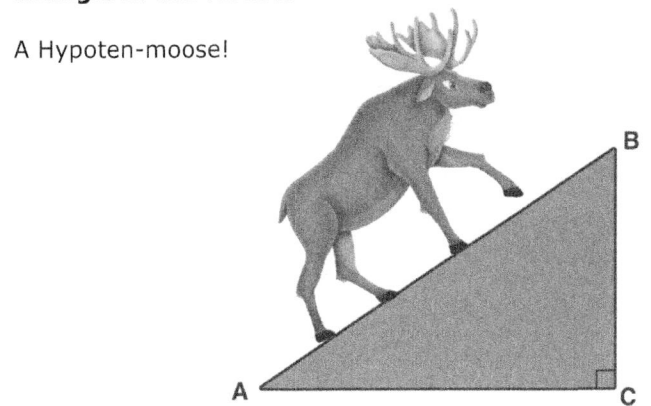

A Hypoten-moose!

111.) Why was the triangle so cold?

Because he was ice-sosceles.

112.) What triangle should you avoid at all costs?

The Bermuda Triangle!

113.) What did the overweight square say to his girlfriend?

I'm feeling a bit out of shape!

114.) What do you call a four-sided figure with four equal sides and four right angles in Antarctica?

A Polar square!

115.) What do you call a four-sided figure with four equal sides and four right angles in Canada?

A Grizzly square!

116.) What do you call a four-sided figure with four equal sides and four right angles in Australia?

A Koala square!

117.) What do you call a four-sided figure with four equal sides and four right angles in China?

A Panda square!

118.) What do you call a four-sided glazed donut with four equal sides and four right angles?

A square claw!

WATCH OUT FOR SQUARES!

Silly Mathematicians

119.) What state did the mathematician move to?

Math-achusetts

120.) What happened to the mathematician who was caught robbing banks?

A judge sent him to *prism*.

121.) What do mathematicians like to do after it snows?

Make snow *angles*!

122.) How do mathematicians prefer to eat ice cream?

By moving from pint A to pint B.

123.) What do you call dudes who love math?

Alge-bros!

124.) What is the loudest mathematical operation?

Gong-Division!

125.) What mathematical operation is an Olympic sport?

Ping Pong-Division

126.) What is the most musical mathematical operation?

Song-Division

127.) There are three types of mathematicians...

Those who can count and those who can't!

128.) Why did the math student insist on sitting on the floor while working on multiplication problems?

To prove that she didn't need to use tables!

129.) What is a mathematician's favorite type of carpet?

An area rug!

130.) What is a mathematician's favorite section of New York City?

Times Squared

131.) Did you hear what happened to the statistician on his way to work?

Probably

132.) What do mathematicians eat for dinner on March 14th?

Chicken Pot Pi

133.) A mathematician calls a pizzeria...

Mathematician: How many pizzas can I purchase for immediate delivery?

Pizzeria Owner: Right now, we have six pizzas ready for delivery, but we can make more. How many do you want?

Mathematician: I need ten times what you currently have available! How long is that going to take?

Pizzeria Owner: Well, my friend, it's going to take a while to deliver an *order of magnitude* like that!

134.) Pizza Pie Chart!

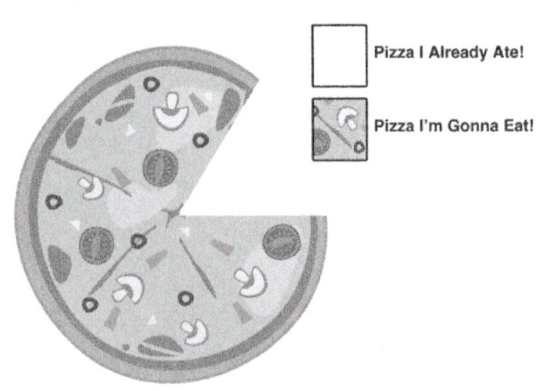

Pizza I Already Ate!

Pizza I'm Gonna Eat!

135.) Why are algebra teachers great dancers?

Because they have algo-rhythm

136.) How are mathematicians similar to the Air Force?

They both rely on using *pi* lots!

137.) In the cafeteria:

Gym Teacher: Does anyone want half of my lunch?

Math Teacher: No thanks, it looks odd to me!

138.) Why did the mathematician's friend get upset when she told him he was average?

Because it was a *mean* thing to say!

You have a central tendency to be rude!

139.) What is Mother Nature's favorite type of graph?

A stem-and-leaf plot

140.) What is a cat's favorite type of graph?

A box-and-whisker plot

141.) What is a baker's favorite type of graph?

A pie chart!

142.) What is a weightlifters favorite type of graph?

A bar graph!

143.) Why do algebra teachers feel superior to geometry teachers?

Because geometry teachers are too *symbol minded*!

144.) Why is a world where geometry doesn't exist a math teacher's worst nightmare?

Because life would be pointless.

145.) What is a mathematician's favorite type of tree?

A Geometree!

Did you know that they have square roots?

146.) The problem with negatives...

I'm not very good at math.

In fact, I find negative numbers so hard to understand that I will stop at nothing to avoid them!

147.) What is a mathematician's favorite chocolate drink?

Ellipse-tine

148.) Why do so many mathematicians wear glasses?

Because it improves *division*

149.) How did the mathematician teach his pet chicken how to do long division?

By showing it lots of egg-samples!

150.) Why did the math teacher only teach her students how to perform subtraction?

Because she wanted to make a difference.

151.) Why should you never trust a mathematician with graph paper?

Because he's definitely plotting something!

152.) Why did Pythagoras and Albert Einstein go to small claims court?

Because they both claimed ownership of C squared.

Wow, you've almost made it to the end of the book.

Very impressive!

(Most people have laughed themselves into a stupor by now.)

Let's see if you're ready for some bonus holiday-themed math jokes...

Holiday Math Jokes

153.) Have you ever heard of the famous Valentine's Day Math Theorem?

YOU + ME = US

154.) What do you get when you divide the the circumference of a jack-o-lantern by its diameter?

Pumpkin Pi

155.) Can monsters be good at mathematics?

Only if you Count Dracula!

156.) Happy Thanksgiving!

...and remember, eating too much pi will give you a large circumference!

157.) Tis The Season To Be Jolly!

158.) Where does a Christmas Tree sit on a number line?

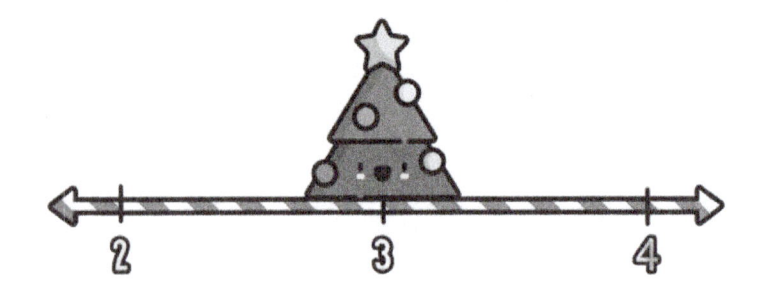

Between a Christmas Two and a Christmas Four!

48

159.) How does Santa Claus use math to save time?

$(Ho)^3$

160.) Where is the best place on Earth to practice multiplication and celebrate New Years Eve?

Times Square!

The End!

Why are you so happy?
The end is coming! No joke. It can be mathematically proven!
OMG! Really?
Yes! It's happening right now. The end of this book is here!

About MashUp Math

MashUp Math is your go-to source for resources, activities, and ideas for making math education fun and exciting for your kids every day! Whether you're looking for lesson plan ideas, free resources, puzzles, and worksheets, video lessons, research and insights, or to connect with other educators, you will always find something cool, fun, and useful at www.mashupmath.com!

Looking for free daily resources, math puzzles, fun ideas, and more? Follow us on social media!

This book is a production of Mashup Math *LLC*.

All rights reserved.

Contact: Please visit **www.mashupmath.com/contact-us** to submit an inquiry.

Copyright Information:

All Mashup Math resources (free and paid) are solely for the purposes of Personal Instruction and Presentation, which purposes include classroom instruction or personal tutoring and creation and use of instructional examples, classwork assignments, homework assignments, tests, and quizzes ("Approved Purposes"). "Personal Instruction and Presentation" means instruction rendered by a teacher to a student either in person or via direct communication methods including but not limited to email, telephone, and video or audio chat (e.g. Skype). Except as otherwise permitted by a Mashup Math representative, you shall not distribute, publicly display, or otherwise make available any worksheets or other Mashup Math materials without the express permission of Mashup Math.

Printed in Great Britain
by Amazon